feeling ALL the feelings

workbook

A Kids' Guide to Exploring Emotions

Brad Petersen

bala kids

illustrated by
Betsy Petersen

How Are You Feeling?!

Welcome!

hello friends !

How are you feeling?

Happy, sad, angry? Or maybe something else you can't quite name. Maybe a mixture of several feelings? Whatever you're feeling, this book is here to help.

We care about feelings, and it's okay to feel all different types of emotions. We also believe the more you learn about feelings, the more feelings you can feel. This is important for helping you understand more about yourself and others.

Have you ever felt down but not known what to do? Or maybe you've had a friend acting sad and you didn't know how to connect with them? We hope this book answers these questions and many others! Not only that, but we also hope you enjoy the fun illustrations, activities, and journal opportunities. The book is organized by feeling. You can simply choose a feeling and hop on over to explore and learn more. Or you can start at the beginning and work your way through!

Happy exploring,

Betsy + Brad

Calm

What Is It?

Calm is a feeling of peace. Think of a time when everything is still and quiet outside—an early spring morning with the dew on the grass, or a silent winter night as snow falls all around. Calm helps you center yourself and find a pathway forward during tough times.

Why Is It Helpful?

Feeling calm can help you decrease your stress and fear. Feeling calm also helps you make better choices. If someone around you feels scared, your calm presence can help them feel safe.

How Do I Recognize It?

It's not always easy to recognize the feeling of calm. You may feel it when you meditate, spend time in nature, or hang out with friends. You'll notice your heart beats more slowly and your breathing and muscles are relaxed. You don't feel worried. You might even be smiling!

Calm as a Cat

Cats can purr to show they feel safe and calm—or to help soothe themselves and make them feel more relaxed when they're worried.

What are three things you can do to help feel calm?

1. _____

2. _____

3. _____

WHAT ABOUT WORRIES?

Calming the Storm

Sometimes our worries stop us from feeling calm. Have you ever been worried before? Lots of things can worry us: our school, the news, the weather, or even what we're supposed to eat for dinner.

Draw or write something that has made you feel worried.

Calm AND Worried?!

Is it possible to feel calm if you're also worried about something? Yes! You can work on accepting your worries and feeling calm at the same time. You can allow your mind to focus on worries and also train it not to get stuck stressing out about any worry longer than you need it to. Now that you've written down some worries, which is bigger—you or the worry? You can take control of the worry and even scribble it out!

TRY THIS!

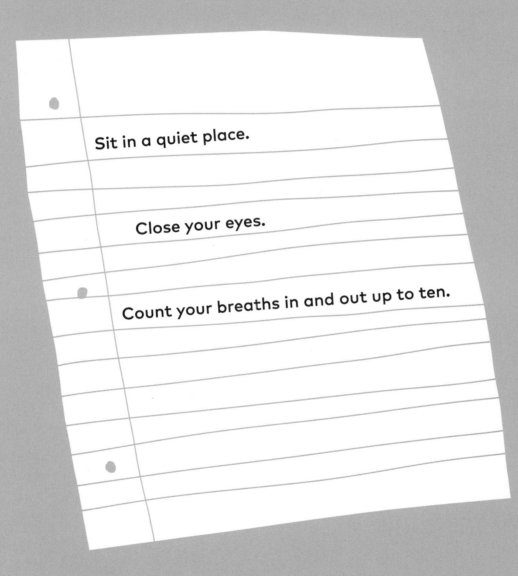

Sit in a quiet place.

Close your eyes.

Count your breaths in and out up to ten.

Once you reach ten, let your mind wander and watch any thoughts and worries roll like waves. After thirty seconds, count your breaths again. This can calm your body while also teaching your mind it's okay to have worries.

Happy

What Is It?

Happiness is that feeling that things are going your way. You feel joy, positivity, and excitement.

Why Is It Helpful?

Everyone deserves to have fun, happy feelings. Feeling happy can help increase your excitement to help others, work on new ideas, and even just relax. It's okay if you don't feel happy all the time, but it's important to make sure you can feel happy sometimes. We don't know everything about happiness in the brain, but we know that the brain relies on moments of happiness to produce certain chemicals important to feeling healthy and good.

How Do I Recognize It?

Happiness makes you want to smile. You feel a swelling in your chest. You feel lighter than air and you don't focus on worries or stress.

Pie Chart Parts of Life

In this activity, you're going to think about happiness in the different parts of your life. We have a few pie charts here with different areas. Just like the example, color in each section depending on how highly you rate your current happiness in that area. For example, if you're 100 percent happy with school, color it in all the way! If you're only 75 percent happy with school, color it in about three-quarters. You can work on these at different times and note how your feelings change over time!

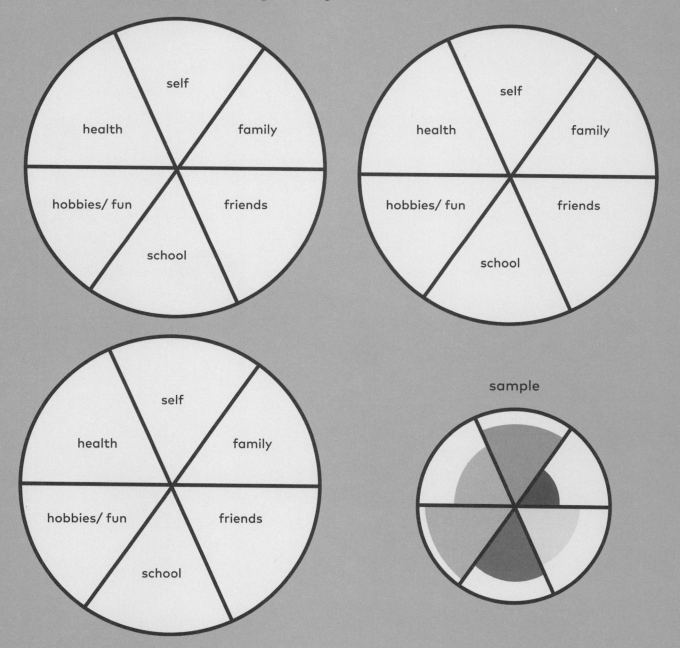

sample

Make Anything Happy with Creativity

Use your creativity to design some happy creatures out of these shapes. Add eyes, arms, legs, a hat, a mustache—whatever you think would make them happy!

Make Your Own Happy Place

Draw your own happy place. A happy place is somewhere real or imaginary where you can feel safe and content. It can be a dream home, a new school, a tree house, or anything you can imagine.

Sad

What Is It?

Sadness is a gloomy, down feeling that might be related to a disappointment, loss, or bump in the road. If you feel sad for long periods of time or all the time, it's important to talk to a grown-up for additional support.

Why Is It Helpful?

It's okay to feel sad sometimes—we all do. It's an important way for your body to slow down and pay attention to what matters most in your life. Feeling sad can help you realize that something didn't go as you planned. It can also help you realize your feelings of care and love for others, such as when you miss someone. Feeling sad all the time can be something serious to talk about with a grown-up, but some sadness here and there is definitely okay and a healthy part of life.

How Do I Recognize It?

You might slow down, cry, slump your shoulders, or want to curl up in bed. Sadness might feel like a pounding heart, heavy breathing, or even a stomachache.

Sadness Storm

Sometimes when you feel sad about one thing, you may start to feel sad about other things as well. It's almost as if there is a rainstorm of sadness, with each raindrop representing a different reason to feel sad. When this happens, it can help to recognize what each raindrop represents for you. When you recognize and name the drops of sadness, you can then begin to address them and heal.

Next time you're feeling sad, write next to each raindrop a reason for your sadness. Once you're done, remind yourself that the rain brings life into the world, helping plants to grow and turning the grass green. These sad feelings will make you fuller of life and strength eventually, even though it feels like a storm in the moment.

Sadness Silver Lining

When we reflect on our experiences, we grow and learn how to better approach them in the future. From our previous sad experiences, for example, there can be a silver lining. Let's take a moment to reflect on a time you felt sad and see what you learn.

What were you sad about?

When did you start to feel that way?

How did your body feel?

Is there something
you have learned
from sadness?

Fun

What Is It?

Fun is the feeling of enjoyment, amusement, or entertainment. You can feel like you're having fun during an experience or even after enjoying an experience as you relive the memories.

Why Is It Helpful?

When you have fun, your levels of stress and anxiety go down. You can learn and play more easily, and you might even make new friends. Everyone deserves the chance to have fun—even grown-ups!

How Do I Recognize It?

You know you're having fun when time seems to fly by much quicker than usual. You smile and laugh, or you might have a deep focus and get in the "flow." You'll probably want to repeat whatever it is that brought you these feelings.

Fun Favorites

What are your three favorite things to do for fun?

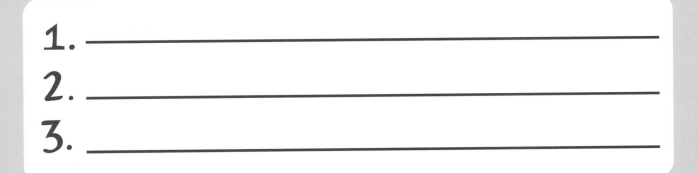

1. ———————————————
2. ———————————————
3. ———————————————

Fun Zone

This is the fun zone!!! Circle your top three most fun modes of transportation:

Challenge: Draw your own fun zone. Is it a picture of your room? Your school? The park? What kinds of things do people do for fun? If you can brainstorm ten or more, you're a legend.

Fun Libs

It was a _____ day in the town of _____ .
adjective   noun

A person named _____ ran _____ to get out
noun   adverb

the door because they were late for class. "Don't forget

your _____!" yelled their mom from inside. "You'll need
noun

it to _____ to Aunt Pattie's later today!" They
verb

grabbed it and said back to their mom, "Don't _____ ,
verb

I got the _____ , and it smells _____!"
noun   adjective

> noun: a person, place, or thing
> adjective: describes a person, place, or thing
> verb: action word
> adverb: describes an action word

Disappointed

What Is It?

Disappointment is when you feel let down that things didn't go as you hoped or planned. Your hopes or dreams didn't come true.

Why Is It Helpful?

Disappointment helps you recognize the joy you feel when your hopes or dreams do come true! It's okay to feel disappointed—we all do sometimes. It allows us to feel humble and human.

How Do I Recognize It?

You might have really looked forward to something or hoped for something and then it didn't work out. The agonizing, dark feeling you experienced is disappointment.

oh no...

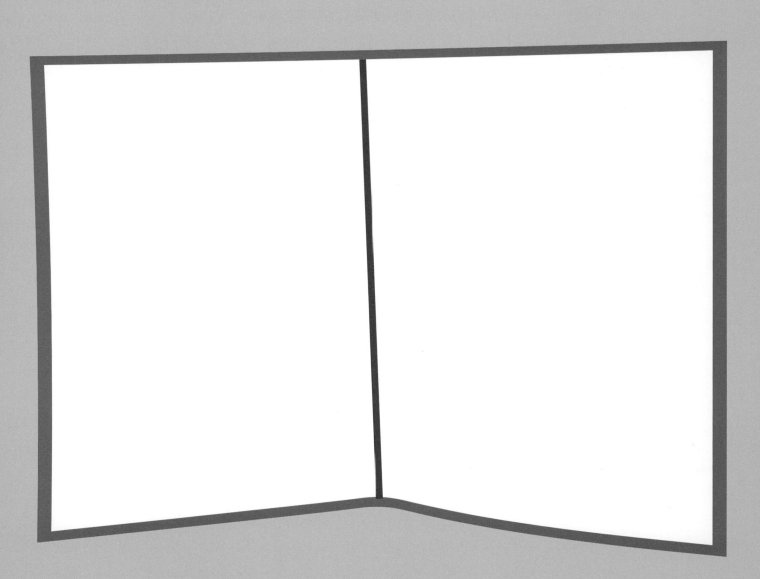

Disappointment Diary

Sometimes it helps to work your way through a disappointment by writing about what happened. Here is some space for you to write about a big disappointment. What happened?

What I Wanted to Happen versus What Actually Happened

Disappointment can come from when something unexpected happens in your life. Below, compare times you felt disappointed by writing or drawing what you wanted to happen and then writing or drawing what actually happened.

WHAT I WANTED

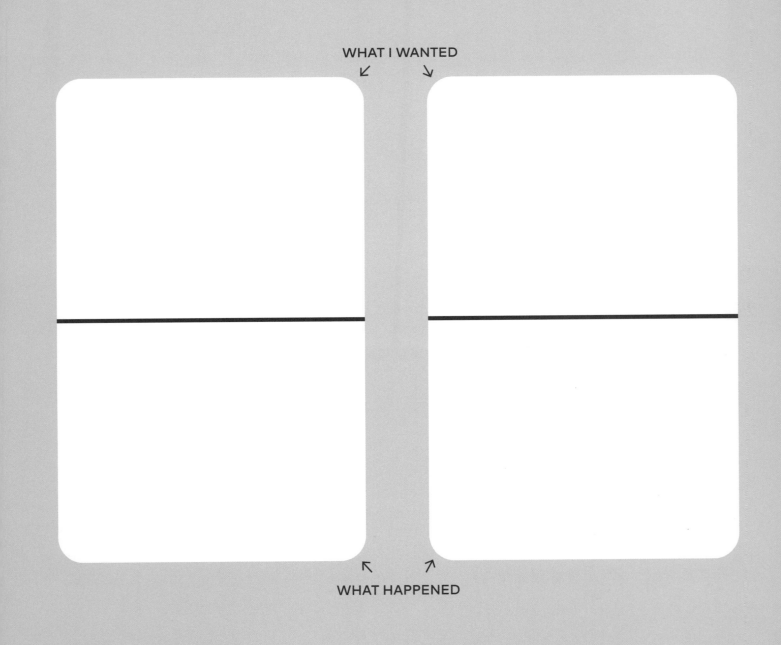

WHAT HAPPENED

When you do this, you can see your life from above, like you're an airplane in the sky. We don't have control over everything in our lives, and it's okay to feel disappointed when things don't go as planned.

WHAT I WANTED

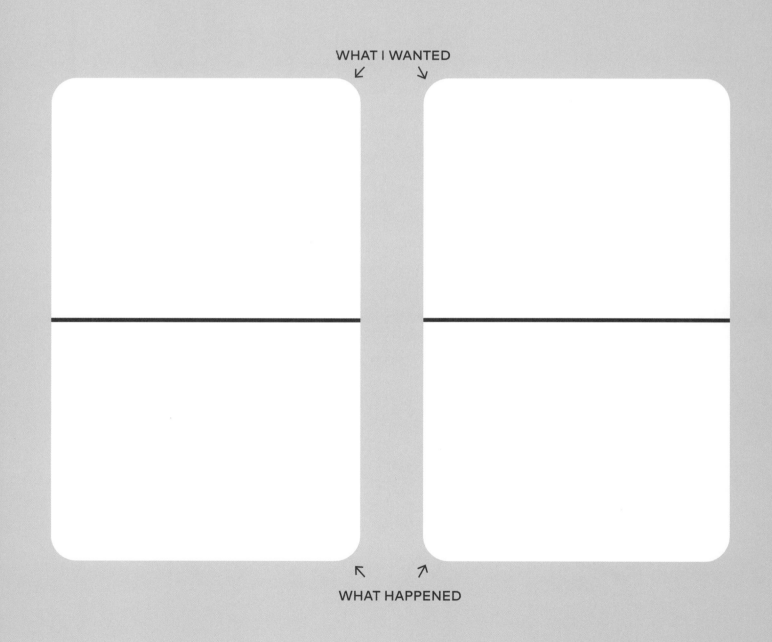

WHAT HAPPENED

Bored

What Is It?

Boredom is whenever you feel like there's nothing to do or you're not interested in what's going on.

Why Is It Helpful?

Boredom isn't good or bad—it's how you react when you're bored that is most important. Developing a plan for when you're bored can make it something excellent! When you feel bored, you know that's a time you can have some fun.

How Do I Recognize It?

Have you ever been someplace and daydreamed you were somewhere else? Have you ever wished you could be doing something, anything, other than what's going on around you? Maybe you lie on the floor, arms and legs spread out, and roll your eyes. Yep, these can be signs that you're bored!

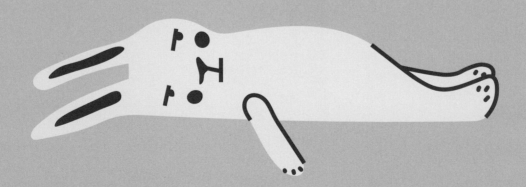

Bored Squiggle

Use this page to start sketching and squiggling when you feel bored. See if you can find something fun to do or create a new idea out of your sketches!

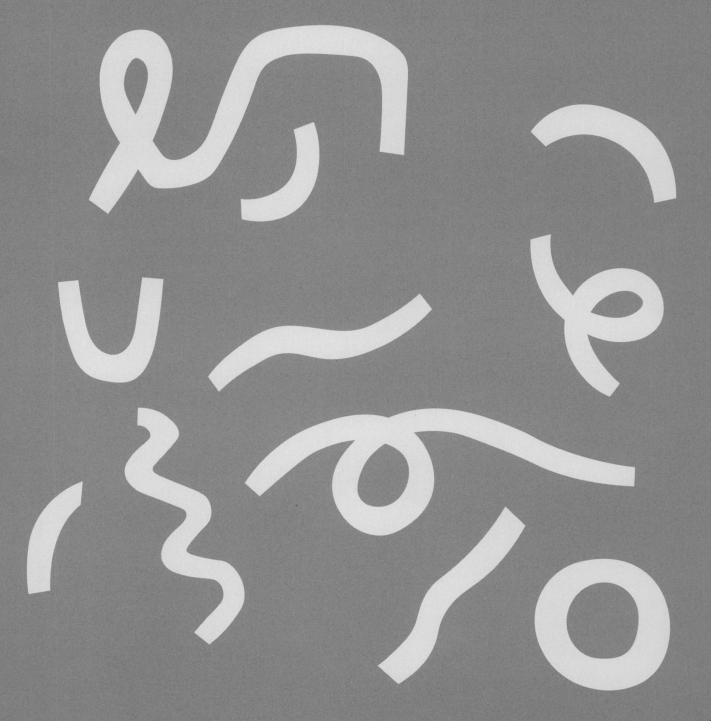

Beating Boredom

Let's work on some fun ideas together now, so you have a list ready next time you feel boredom start to creep up on you.

Use this space to create some ideas for future fun:

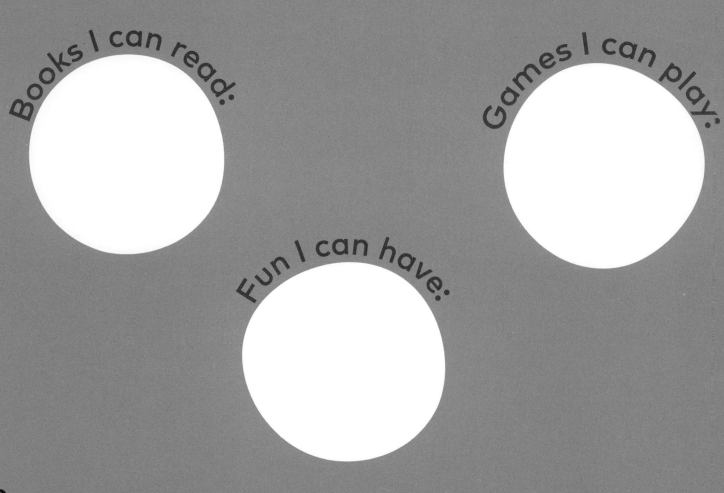

Books I can read:

Games I can play:

Fun I can have:

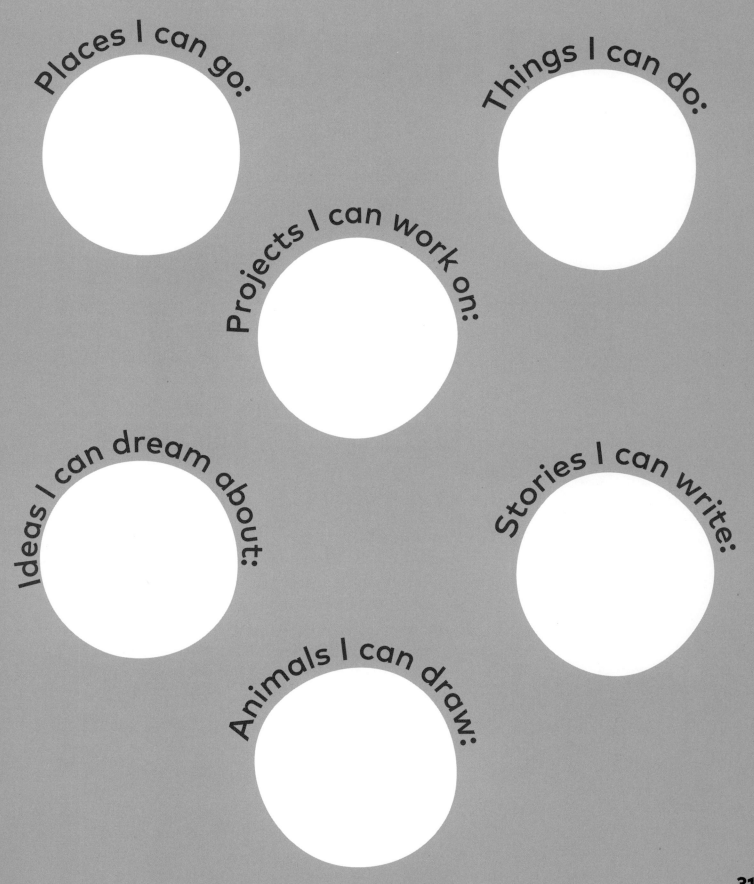

Places I can go:

Things I can do:

Projects I can work on:

Ideas I can dream about:

Stories I can write:

Animals I can draw:

Confident

What Is It?

Feeling confident means that you believe in yourself and feel good about how you can approach any particular moment. It doesn't necessarily mean you think you're better than others, just that you think you can be your best version of yourself!

Why Is It Helpful?

We all have that little thought inside our heads telling us we can't do certain things or don't deserve to feel confident about a big challenge. Building your confidence helps you overcome these feelings of self-doubt. Confidence is important because you're special, unique, and the only you in the whole world.

How Do I Recognize It?

Feeling confident starts with accepting yourself as a beautiful, unique, special person. This means you don't talk negatively about yourself in your mind or out loud. You can also practice self-care and self-love. Every day, get in a good routine that you feel comfortable with. Spend time with people that lift you up and make you feel good about yourself. When you confront a tough challenge, you will notice an inner voice and feeling cheering you on. You can do it!

Confidence List

Even if we aren't Olympic athletes or famous inventors, we have all done things we feel proud of that boost our confidence. For example, if you've painted a painting at school, the next time someone asks you to paint something, you can feel confident because you've had experience doing it before. Brainstorm a list of your accomplishments to boost your confidence for future challenges. Below, write or draw ten things you've done before that make you feel proud of yourself.

1. _____

2. _____

3. _____

4. _____

5. _____

6. _____

7. _____

8. _____

9. _____

10. _____

If you're prepared, you can feel confident
you can accomplish your goals.

Angry

What Is It?

Anger is a strong feeling of dislike toward something or someone. It's similar to feeling mad or furious, and can feel like smoke is pouring out of your ears.

Why Is It Helpful?

Anger is a way for your body to deal with things it doesn't like. You might have a physical or emotional reaction that leads to anger, which is a way to loosen the tension in your body. Learning to channel your anger to calm your nerves can be a helpful, healthy part of life!

How Do I Recognize It?

Underneath anger we often have the feelings of fear and sadness. You might want to act out when you're feeling angry, which is a way to handle those feelings of fear, stress, or sadness. Properly channeling anger can be an important way for you to cope with these emotions. Everyone gets angry, and it comes and goes.

Draw what it feels like inside when you're angry.

The Fable of the Ant and the Angry Armadillo

Once, an armadillo wandered down the path toward the pond for a drink. The day was hot, and the armadillo felt thirstier than ever before. When she arrived at the pond, she noticed a long line of thirsty ants waiting their turn.

"Oh no," she thought. "I'm so thirsty, I can't wait behind all these tiny ants!"

She decided to try an old trick—curl up into a ball, then roll down the hill past the ants right into the pond. "I will get my drink soon," she thought.

So, she rolled up and started bouncing down the hill toward the pond.

Right before she reached the water's edge, someone cried out, "STOP!!!" and she screeched to a halt, crashing into a bush.

Dizzily looking around, she felt so angry. How dare someone make her stop and crash into a bush! She shook her head, furious, wanting to find out who it was.

"You should be more careful," a little ant squeaked up to the angry armadillo.

"Why!?" grumbled the armadillo. "I'm thirstier than a camel! I need to get down to that pond!"

"Well," the ant said, "we're all thirsty, but you almost squashed all our little ant kids up ahead. You probably didn't see them from far away, but they're about to have their turn to drink. If I hadn't told you to stop, they'd all be flatter than pancakes!"

"Oh," said the armadillo, "I'm terribly sorry—I had no idea!" She felt bad. She never wanted to squash anyone. Her anger turned to embarrassment as she walked back to the end of the line. Soon enough, she got her turn and was able to get a nice long drink. She apologized to the ants and never rolled down the hill into the pond again.

Sometimes anger and impatience are related. If we're able to build up our patience and have empathy for others, we can calm our anger and treat others with kindness.

Anger Thermometer

We feel all types and kinds of anger. This thermometer is here to help you describe just how angry you feel. You can use it to share with others how you're feeling.

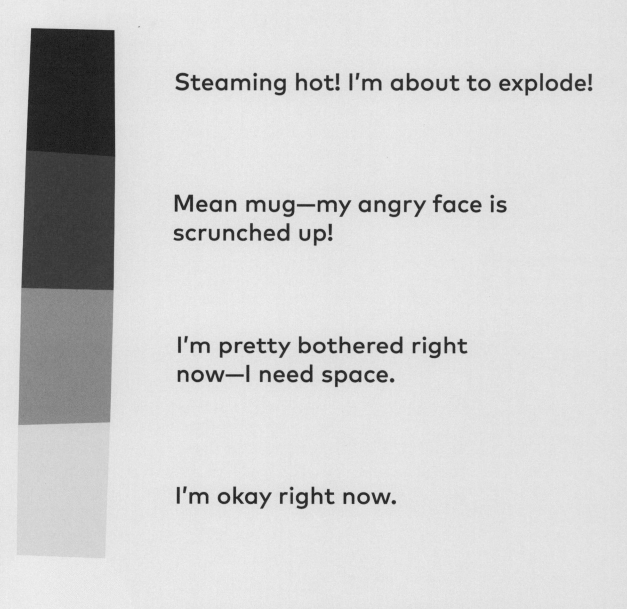

Steaming hot! I'm about to explode!

Mean mug—my angry face is scrunched up!

I'm pretty bothered right now—I need space.

I'm okay right now.

I'm super calm and feeling peaceful.

Patient

What Is It?

Patience is the ability to keep your cool and stay calm in challenging, difficult, or stressful situations.

Why Is It Helpful?

It's true, sometimes we feel the opposite of patient—impatient It's a constant struggle to balance the desire to have what we want right now with calmly waiting. If we feel patient, we will feel less anxious, less stressed, and more open to new experiences. You don't *have* to feel patient—but give it a try!

How Do I Recognize It?

Sometimes you might recognize patience when working with other people—maybe when helping someone younger than you to learn a new skill or waiting for them to catch up to you. You want to hurry up and be done with everything, but you take a deep breath and slow down for them to work at their own pace. You might also recognize this feeling when you decide to wait for something you want (like dessert!) until the right time (after dinner!).

Patiently Persistent—Heron

The great blue heron is a patiently persistent animal. To catch its prey, it stands perfectly still for long periods of time before finding the best moment to strike.

You can learn from the heron and be patiently persistent. If there is something you want but can't have at this exact moment, you can practice patience while waiting for the perfect moment. For example, if you wish you could go for a walk outside but it's not the best weather, you can patiently watch the weather for the right time, when it's best to go out and about.

Being Breezy Isn't Easy

Looking back on times when you felt patient will help you see where patience comes more easily for you. And recognizing times you felt impatient rather than patient will help you identify where you can focus some energy on building more patience.

Below, draw or write about three times you showed great patience.

Now draw or write about three times you did not show great patience.

Patience Takes Practice

Build up your patience and mindfulness with this simple practice. Trace the circle as best you can, beginning on the outside all the way down to the tiny inside. Then reverse and go all the way back out. Notice your thoughts and feelings concentrating, guiding you through the process. You're building your patience!

Fearful

What Is It?

Fear is a feeling that something scary or dangerous might pose a threat to your safety. It's a feeling that makes you want to seek comfort, routine, and maybe even shelter. Sometimes you want to hide when you're feeling afraid.

Why Is It Helpful?

We shouldn't be afraid of anything, right? Wrong! It's the brain's way of trying to protect us from danger. We've developed fear as a useful emotion to help us stay safe and make better choices. That said, there are some things we can learn to fear less—like eating broccoli.

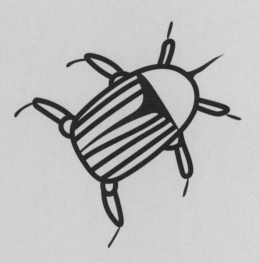

How Do I Recognize It?

Some things we all fear, especially when we're kids. It's totally normal! Bugs, heights, loud noises, going to the doctor, imaginary monsters, and the dark—they can all be scary! It's important to recognize that we all feel scared about these things, but not to dwell on them. And you can plan to build up your bravery.

Fear Thought Process

1.

Listen to the thought and picture the scary thing in your mind.

2.

Decide if the fear is realistic or not realistic.

3.

What evidence do you have to support or disprove it?

4.

Challenge the thought and tell it to go away.

EXAMPLE

1. I'm afraid when my parents leave.
2. The fear is probably not really going to happen.
3. Every other time my parents left, they came back safely.
4. Since it isn't real, I'm not going to let it control my thoughts.

Overcoming Fear with Mindfulness

A mindfulness grounding practice can help you overcome fear in the moment. Here are three grounding practices you can try when you start to feel afraid.

3, 2, 1 Senses

3 things you can see
2 things you can hear
1 thing you can smell

Strong as a Tree

Stand up and imagine you're a tree. Feel the weight of your feet on the ground. Notice the top of your head reaching up to the sky. Imagine your arms as branches—reach them out into the world.

Safe Space

Wrap your arms around yourself in a hug and repeat the phrase, "I am safe in this space."

Heartbeat

Did you know that listening to someone else's heartbeat can calm you down? Try it next time you feel afraid. Does it work for you?

Jealous

What Is It?

Jealousy is a feeling of anger or resentment that someone has something that you don't. Often our jealousy is more a feeling we feel about ourselves rather than what we feel about others. This can especially be true with our siblings or family members.

Why Is It Helpful?

Feeling jealous can help you grow your gratitude for the things you do have, if you can realize the feeling and reflect on your experience. Do you feel okay with who you are or what you have? How can you try to make it right when you and someone else don't get along because of jealousy?

How Do I Recognize It?

You can recognize feelings of jealousy when you feel insecure or lacking when comparing yourself to someone else. You might also experience FOMO, the fear of missing out! When you feel these types of feelings, or when you feel angry that someone has some type of experience or strength that you don't see in yourself, those types of feelings are related to jealousy.

Friends Again

Let's say your sibling or friend gets a new toy you really wish you had. You might feel a bit jealous! What if it affects your friendship? What if they brag about it and it makes you mad? If you're friends at first, you can be friends again. Talk it out, take a break, or walk away for a time. It's not worth ending your friendship over a small thing!

TALK IT OUT

TAKE A BREAK

WALK AWAY

Jealous Friends

Two hedgehogs were walking home after eating a tasty lunch in the woods. One of the hedgehogs, Maria, had the softest, shiniest quills in town, and everyone admired them. For the other hedgehog, Jada, her quills were sharp and hard. No one ever complimented her on their texture or shine. Usually that didn't bother her, but today she was feeling slightly jealous. Maria had landed the star role in the school play, and everyone knew it was because she was the shiniest and softest in class.

While they walked, Maria bragged about her shiny quills and showed Jada how they gleamed in the sunlight. Unfortunately, all that shine and gleam attracted the eyes of the ever-watchful Mr. Coyote. He leaped out from behind the bushes and drooled at the sight of the soft, luscious quills, which would pose no threat to his sharp teeth and claws. Mr. Coyote leaped out toward Maria. Suddenly Jada curled into a ball and bounced in front of Maria. Terrified by her pointy, sharp quills, Mr. Coyote shifted direction and narrowly escaped a painful fate. He ran into the woods howling in frustration.

Maria thanked Jada and wondered where she might be without those sharp, bristly quills.

And thus we see that each person's unique qualities are important in their own special ways.

Jealousy Diagnosis

SIGNS

Walking around mad, pouting, ignoring fun activities, and not wanting to spend time with others

SYMPTOMS

Angry at your friend, frustrated that you don't have something, wishing you were different somehow

TREATMENT

Work on a gratitude journal, talk it out with your friend, take a break somewhere quiet, make a list of everything you're good at

Diagnose something you've felt jealous about. Fill out this clipboard with your own symptoms and treatment to see if your recommendations work the next time these feelings come about!

Generous

What Is It?

Generosity means that you want to give what you have to help others.

Why Is It Helpful?

Generosity is something special that builds friendships and makes your community a better place. Sometimes you're the one feeling generous, and you make someone else's day. Other times, someone acts with generosity toward you, and it's the highlight of your week!

How Do I Recognize It?

When you're willing to share anything you have with others—your time, kindness, money, toys, or anything else—you're feeling generous. Do you know someone who has a "generous spirit," someone who always feels this way and seeks to help those around them through their generosity?

Building a Generous Spirit

Use this template to construct a more generous spirit. Each of the tools below is something you can use to become more generous. Try your best to draw or write your answers in the blank spaces.

What do you have that you can share with others?

Who would you like to share something with?

Tell about a time someone shared something with you.

When would you like to share something with someone?

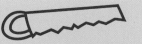

What is something kind you can do for someone else?

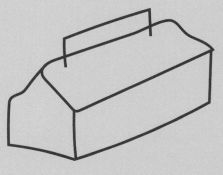

Gift Giving

You've been assigned to share the absolute coolest surprises with your friend. Use your best craftsmanship to draw what you might give this friend to make them happy. It can be as amazing or imaginative as possible!

```
C F U N T C A R I N G K B L N
H E A R T B E A T T A T J Z W
L E W C O M P A S S I O N Z I
V K L H U R R A Y O C G I G S
W J D K C L O V E K A E C Y H
C U T E A B F F S A L T E X A
K A S H A R I N G Y M H D I B
I C B R A V E O M T M E O N T
N O C M E D I T A T E R Y E O
D O L H A P P Y Q L Z N C N G
F L M I N D F U L N E S S V E
G R A T I T U D E U O S P Y T
K J E A L O U S H L W Z L K H
I B T V F R I E N D S M A G E
Y E S Y A N G R Y S N A Y F R
```

Word Search

Mindfulness	Caring	Fun	Love
Compassion	Hurray	Cute	BFFs
Gratitude	Jealous	Play	Calm
Heartbeat	Sharing	Cool	Wish
Meditate	Angry	Brave	Envy
Together	Happy	Yes	Kind
Okay	Nice	Friends	

Generous Notes

Take a few moments to be generous to yourself below. Write three things that you love about yourself!

I'm really good at _____.

I love my _____.

One thing that makes me special is that _____

_____.

How might you respond with generosity to others in the following situations?

Someone gives you a present that you always dreamed about getting.

You meet a new friend and they act a little bit shy.

Someone close to you gets upset and calls you a name.

Self-Portrait—Generous Edition

We're all beautiful in our own way. It's important that we're kind to ourselves and recognize our own inner and outer beauty and strengths. Take a few moments to draw a self-portrait above and show just how wonderful you are.

Generous You

Draw or write how you would show kindness to yourself.

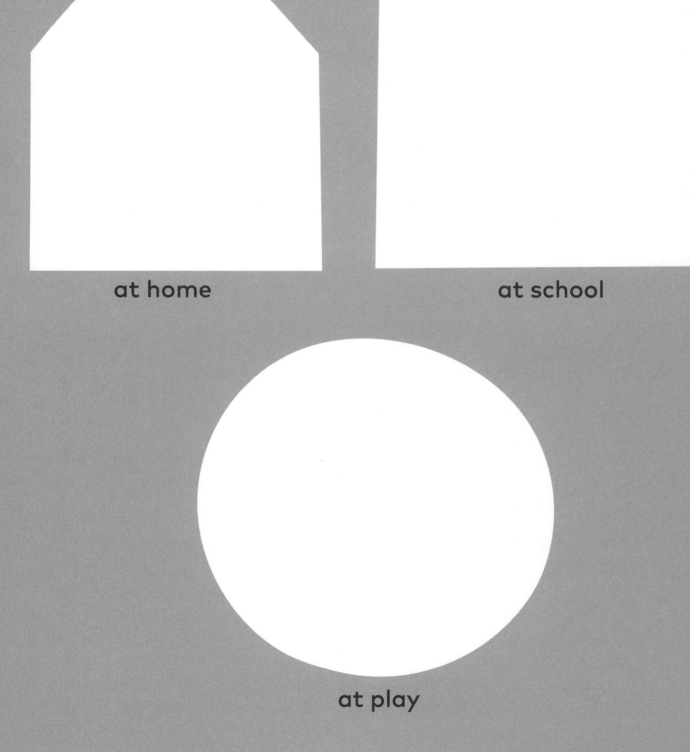

at home

at school

at play

Grouchy

What Is It?

Feeling grouchy is when you have a bad temper mixed with some complaining. You also might be a bit easy to irritate. Some people call it feeling grouchy, others call it grumpy!

Why Is It Helpful?

Expressing grouchiness is a way of communicating your inner feelings. If you feel grouchy because you're hungry, that's a communication that it's time to grab a snack. If you feel grouchy after not sleeping well, you now know you can try to get to bed a little bit earlier.

How Do I Recognize It?

Grouchiness and grumpiness can be related to frustration, anger, or depression. We can be affected by things around us or by just having a bad day. Everyone feels grouchy sometimes—maybe we had a bad sleep, or our plans fell through. If you feel grumpy more often than not, share your feelings with an adult for extra help.

How Can I Help Others Who Feel Grouchy?

Some of us have friends, family, or loved ones who feel grouchy sometimes. Maybe they're working a hard job or not getting enough sleep. Maybe they need some extra alone time. Whatever the case, you can help others who feel grouchy by giving them some extra space, care, and love. Make them a card telling them what you like best about them, offer them a snack, or see if they would like to play a game with you.

Does It Make You Feel Grouchy?

Knowing what might affect your feelings can help you know what you can do to avoid feeling grouchy or to change things around! Color in the charts below to show how grouchy you might feel in the following situations:

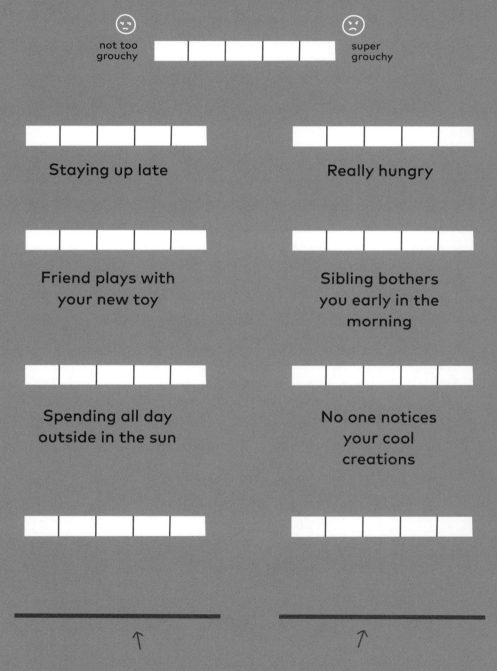

not too grouchy

super grouchy

Staying up late

Really hungry

Friend plays with your new toy

Sibling bothers you early in the morning

Spending all day outside in the sun

No one notices your cool creations

↑

↑

Fill in your own things that make you feel grouchy!

How to Recharge When You're Feeling Grouchy

If you're feeling grouchy or grumpy, here are three ways to recharge to help you turn around your grouchy feelings.

First, you can take a break and rest. Maybe take a nap or have some quiet time on your own in your room or personal space. You can even play with a toy by yourself.

Second, you can take action and turn your feelings around. Get moving: play a game, jump around, or even go for a walk.

Third, you can take care of someone or something. Maybe you have a pet you can brush or a sibling you can help with a project. Maybe you can clean up your room a little bit. Taking care of things will help change the way you're feeling.

Draw or write what some of your plans will be the next time you're feeling grouchy and want to turn things around.

Grateful

What Is It?

Gratitude is a feeling of thanks for people, things, and places in your life. You often feel grateful when you take a moment and reflect on the good, better, and best in your life.

Why Is It Helpful?

Feeling grateful improves your happiness and health. It also helps you have better relationships with those you love and builds your resilience against tough times.

How Do I Recognize It?

Gratitude feels like loving feelings and a warm, fuzzy thankfulness for people or things in your life. It can be tricky to know what exactly you have to feel grateful for apart from the basics. Of course you're grateful for your shelter, food, loved ones, and water. However, you can go deeper. Think about what you would miss if it were gone forever. Your toys? Books? Transportation? Stores? Grass? Trees? The ocean?

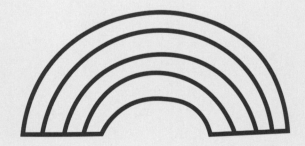

Gratitude is good for your mind, body, feelings, and brain. You can't feel enough gratitude!

Gratitude Game

Here's a fun game to practice gratitude for the people around you. Fill in each of the blank spaces with the name of someone who fits the description in your life.

I love_____because they are as reliable as the sunrise.

I feel grateful for_____because they're as brave as a lion.

_____is the funniest person I know.

When_____treats me with kindness, I know I'm loved.

I enjoy spending time most with_____.

I am grateful for_____because they help me when I'm feeling down.

Gratitude Journal

With this ongoing activity, you can grow your attitude of gratitude in one week of about five minutes per day. Every day, for seven days, use this journal space to write three unique things you feel thankful for. In the end, you will see all the small things you can feel grateful for!

1. _____
2. _____
3. _____

1. _____
2. _____
3. _____

1. _____
2. _____
3. _____

1. _____
2. _____
3. _____

1. _____
2. _____
3. _____

1. _____
2. _____
3. _____

1. _____
2. _____
3. _____

Gratitude Vision

Enter into a mindful state with this gratitude vision activity. Find a quiet place and take about five minutes to make your way through the steps.

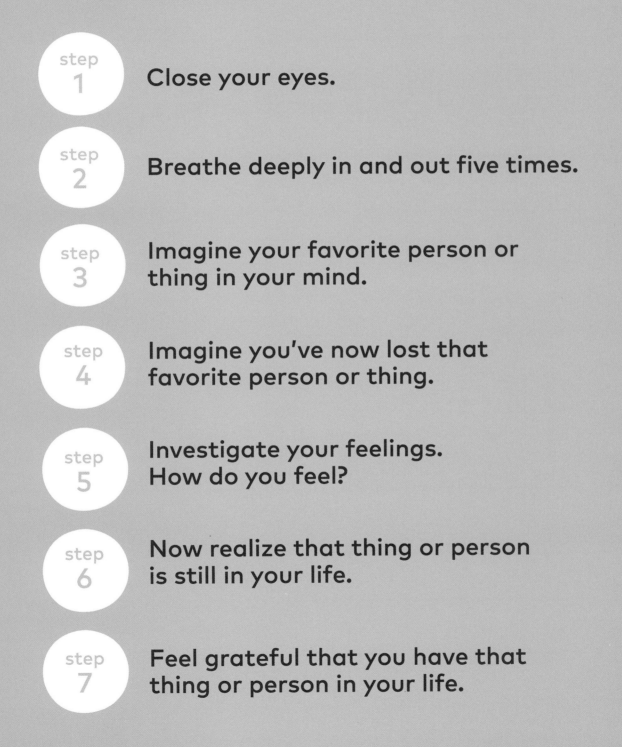

step 1
Close your eyes.

step 2
Breathe deeply in and out five times.

step 3
Imagine your favorite person or thing in your mind.

step 4
Imagine you've now lost that favorite person or thing.

step 5
Investigate your feelings. How do you feel?

step 6
Now realize that thing or person is still in your life.

step 7
Feel grateful that you have that thing or person in your life.

Shaky Shaky

A secret handshake is a great way to glow up any day and show your gratitude for friends. Together with a friend, invent a secret handshake only you will know. Make it as fun and goofy as possible!

Thumb wiggle

Pointy thumb

The wave

Turkey feathers

Brave

What Is It?

Bravery is facing fears with courage—doing the right thing, even when it's difficult or scary. Bravery can be standing up for what's fair. It can be caring for others, trying a new activity, or dancing in the spotlight.

Why Is It Helpful?

Bravery helps you overcome your fears. It helps you help others when the going gets tough. Maybe someone needs help with a group project at school but feels afraid of asking the teacher for help—you can be brave to help them ask!

How Do I Recognize It?

Bravery seems like something larger than life—something daring and exciting. But it's true, anyone can be brave in their own life, however large or small they are. If you're trying to do the right thing in the face of fear, you're acting bravely.

Design Your Own Bravery Awards

Take a moment to design some awards for brave things you've done.
Be sure to include some words or pictures that describe what each
award means to you.

Unexpected Bravery

The animal kingdom has many examples of brave animals we might not expect. For example, pigeons are some of the bravest birds around! Their unusual ability to find their home, even when beginning far away, has led to their use as messengers for humans. Some pigeons have even carried important messages over 150 miles to help their human caregivers in need. Imagine how scary it would be to fly such a distance with such an important job! They bravely get the job done to fly home safely.

Help the messenger pigeon deliver this message!

Write a Letter to Your Future Self

Be brave and ambitious with your goals. No matter who comes and goes in your life, you will always have yourself to care and love. Write a letter to your future self—ask how you're doing. Have you accomplished some of the goals you hope for right now? Who are your friends? What do you like to do for fun? Tell your future self what's going on in your life now, in the present. Describe your feelings. Tell your future self what you hope for. Bonus points for tearing out, folding up, and saving it to open again in the future!

Lonely

What Is It?

Feeling lonely is a particular kind of sadness or down feeling due to missing friends, family, or loved ones. It can also come from feeling alone, even though you might have those people that care about you all around you.

Why Is It Helpful?

No matter how many siblings, friends, or pets someone has, everyone feels lonely sometimes. Even in the animal kingdom, animals can feel lonely. Think about a lone wolf howling in the dark night, lonely for its pack. It's what you decide to do when you're lonely that can help you feel connected and appreciated.

How Do I Recognize It?

Feeling lonely can begin by missing others. If you miss others and no one else is around, it can feel even more isolating. Sometimes if no one is paying attention to you, you can feel lonely even if others are all around you.

HOWWWL!

What Are Some Ways to Make Friends?

Sometimes loneliness can emerge from your environment: Maybe you just moved to a new town. Maybe your best friend just changed schools. Maybe your parent has had to travel for work. In any case, here are some reliable ways to make friends. If you try a few of these, and have an open mind, you might just make a new friend!

Invite someone over to play at your house.

Volunteer to help mentor younger students at your school.

Write a letter to a cousin or faraway friend.

Say sorry when you make a mistake.

Accept invitations to try something new, as long as it's healthy and safe.

Video chat a family member or friend who lives far away.

Use the image bank above to help our friend feel less lonely.

Universal Feelings

Across the universe, everyone feels similarly at times. Whenever you feel lonely, you can know that there are other people in the world feeling the same way. Here are some mantras, or phrases, you can think of to know you're not alone.

 Everyone feels lonely sometimes.

 If someone else were in my position, they would probably feel like I do, too.

 I am a loved and loving human being.

 I can show kindness to myself.

 No feeling lasts forever.

Frustrated

What Is It?

Feeling frustrated is a type of annoyance at not being able to do or get something you would like. You can also feel frustrated when things don't go your way, especially when you're under lots of stress.

Why Is It Helpful?

It's okay to feel frustrated; it's a part of childhood and gets better as you get older. Frustration is your body's way of working through stressful moments. Recognizing frustration and then communicating your feelings with grown-ups and others can help you gain more understanding about yourself and the world around you.

How Do I Recognize It?

You can recognize that you're feeling frustrated when you begin to be bothered by small things that normally aren't a big deal—such as when you try to fix a flat bike tire in the hot sun and it just isn't working out! You can communicate with others to express your feelings. Next time you're feeling frustrated, take some time to write or draw your feelings here, then share them with someone you trust to try to ease some of your frustration.

Frustrating Feelings

What does it look like inside your brain when you're feeling frustrated? Draw or write inside this brain what it looks like for you!

Body Signals

We don't only feel feelings in our brain. We also feel them in our body and how it reacts. With practice, you can identify some of your feelings by listening to your body and how it's reacting. Here is a simple map to help get you started.

HEAD: Headaches can be a sign of stress or anxiety, which can lead to frustration.

NECK: If your neck is feeling tight, it could be a signal that you're worried or stressed.

HEART: If your heart is beating quickly, you might be angry, nervous, or frustrated.

STOMACH: A stomachache could be a signal that you're feeling stressed, anxious, or nervous.

FOOT: If you find your leg or foot constantly tapping, it might be a signal that you're feeling anxious.

Frustration Station

Help the frustrated astronaut figure out which flying objects they will need to bring back on the space station!

Hopeful

What Is It?

Hopeful is an inspiring feeling that things will work out the way you wish. You can feel hopeful for the future, hopeful that you will win a contest, or even hopeful that tomorrow will be better than today. Feeling hopeful is the opposite of feeling hopeless or gloomy.

Why Is It Helpful?

Sometimes you can hope for something and it doesn't work out. This doesn't mean you shouldn't feel hopeful! Practicing feeling hopeful will lead you to experience more happiness and confidence in the future.

How Do I Recognize It?

You know you're feeling hopeful when you feel optimistic about the future and look forward to maybe accomplishing a goal you have. You can have these feelings about small things, such as you hope that it snows tomorrow. You can also feel hopeful about larger things, such as you hope to become a teacher or doctor when you grow up.

Hopeful Thinking

Write down ten things you feel hopeful about.

1. _____

2. _____

3. _____

4. _____

5. _____

6. _____

7. _____

8. _____

9. _____

10. _____

Helping Others Helps Your Hope

When you help others, you can feel more hopeful while also helping those around you feel more hopeful. A small act of kindness can make someone's day and give them an extra nudge of hope for a better, brighter tomorrow. Circle three of the following ways to show kindness and commit to using them to help brighten someone's day!

Say something kind.

Write a note telling someone what they're good at.

Tidy up a room more than usual.

Give someone a small gift.

Invite someone to play.

Ask someone about something that interests them.

Hopeful Hop

Help this clever bunny hop along the path and find their tasty pile of carrots—hopefully you can make it through this tricky maze!

Determined

What Is It?

Feeling determined means you're ready to work toward your goals with persistence in the face of obstacles. You try your best to not give up and give your best effort toward something you care about.

Why Is It Helpful?

Feeling determined acts as a spark to help you accomplish different tasks, jobs, or goals. As you increase your determination, you may surprise yourself at your growth. This feeling is especially helpful for turning things around when you feel down or sad about unexpected events. If you don't make a sports team or your artwork isn't selected for the contest, you can still keep trying and maybe things will work out next time.

How Do I Recognize It?

If you get knocked down while trying to learn a new skateboarding trick, you get back up and keep trying. If you don't get the grade you wanted on an art assignment, you keep trying your best on the next assignment. If an opponent beats you in a chess match, you learn even more about chess and come back ready to play even better the next round!

Mountain Goat Mantra

You can be like this mountain goat and repeat to yourself, "I can do hard things!"

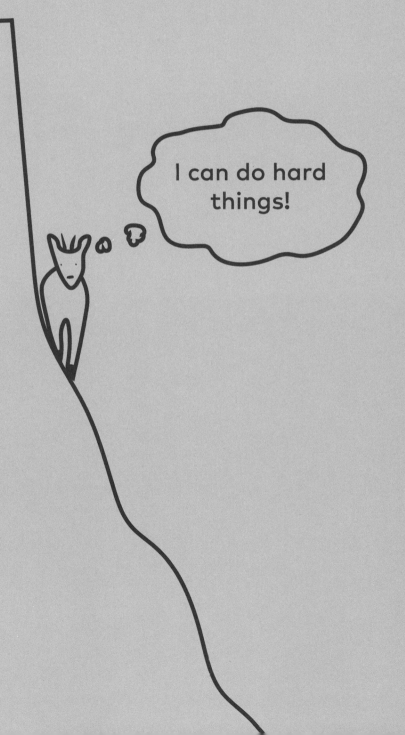

Goal, Set, Match

Take your time here to brainstorm, then write or draw goals you have for the future. They can be goals for far away in the future or for the next couple of years. They should stretch you a little bit, too—not just simple goals you could achieve without working hard.

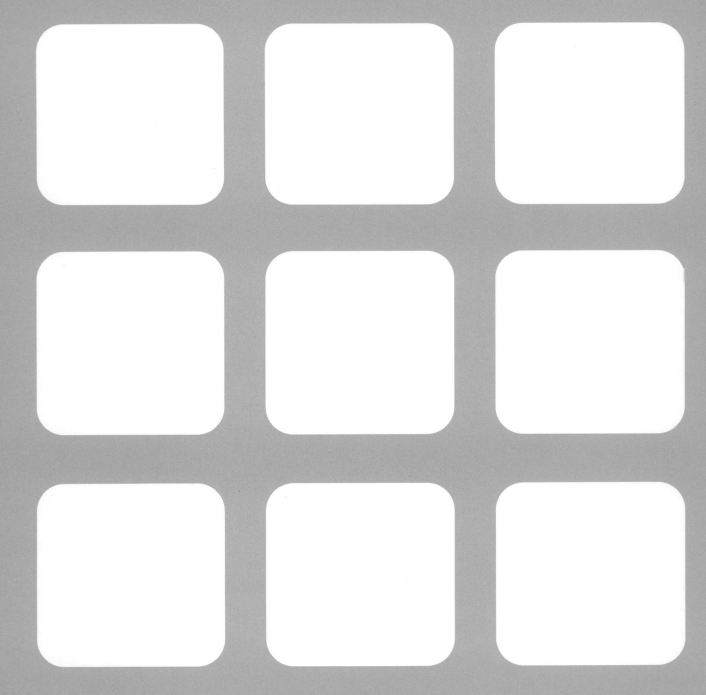

How Are You Feeling?

Add eyebrows and a mouth to show how you feel about these different experiences.

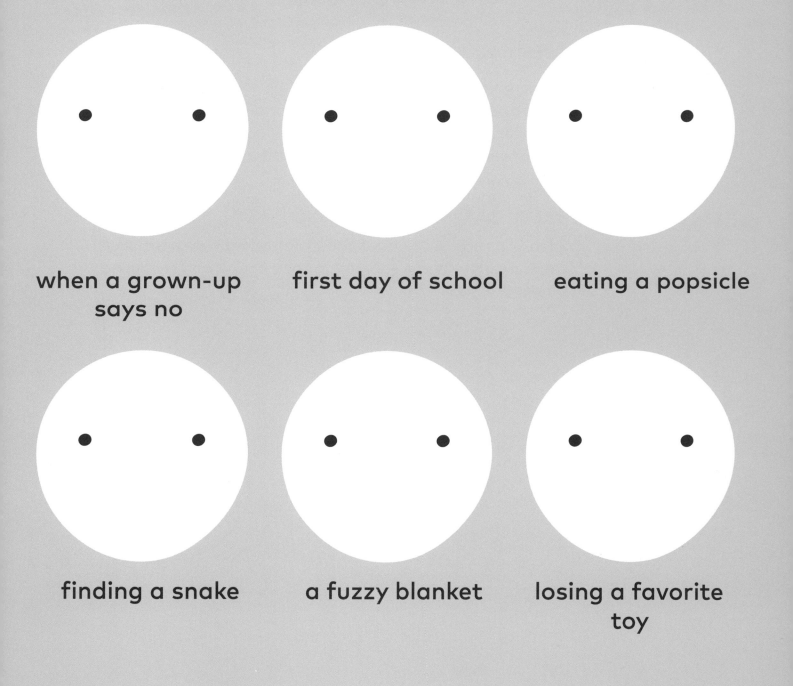

when a grown-up
says no

first day of school

eating a popsicle

finding a snake

a fuzzy blanket

losing a favorite
toy

Empathetic

What Is It?

Empathy is the ability to put yourself in another person's shoes. You can understand and share the feelings of others.

Why Is It Helpful?

Feeling empathetic is important to help you grow closer to others and build a more connected and loving community. This feeling helps you listen to others, see things from their point of view, and build bridges of understanding.

How Do I Recognize It?

When you reflect on your similarities and differences with others and try to put yourself in their shoes, you're feeling empathetic.

Empathetic Flowers

Notice the differences and similarities between all the flowers on this page. What are three differences? What are three similarities?

In the space below, draw some of your own flowers or plants that have some differences and some similarities.

Empathy Camera

A camera uses its lens to focus on objects that are either close or far away. You can use your own imaginary camera to focus on those right around you, making sure you listen and understand them. Also, you can use your imaginary camera to zoom out and consider the wider world and all the different types of people and places that are different from you.

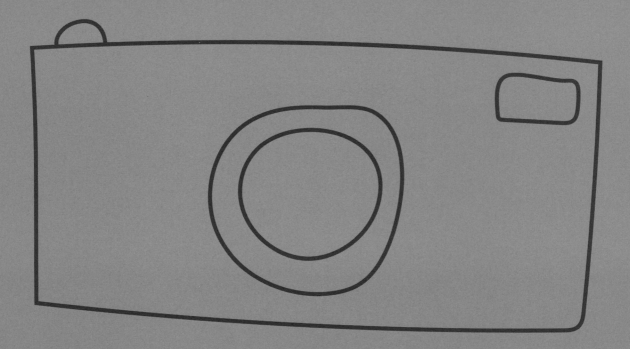

Empathy Letter

Write a letter or draw a picture for a friend or person you care about. Show or tell them some of your similarities and why that makes your friendship special.

How Are You

FEELING?!

Bala Kids
An imprint of Shambhala Publications, Inc.
2129 13th Street
Boulder, Colorado 80302
www.shambhala.com

Cover art: Betsy Petersen
Design by Betsy Petersen and Kara Plikaitis

9 8 7 6 5 4 3 2 1

First Edition
Printed in Singapore

Shambhala Publications makes every effort to
print on acid-free, recycled paper.
Bala Kids is distributed worldwide by Penguin Random House, Inc.,
and its subsidiaries.

ISBN: 978-1-64547-075-5